"Alone we can do so little;
together we can do so much."

–Helen Keller

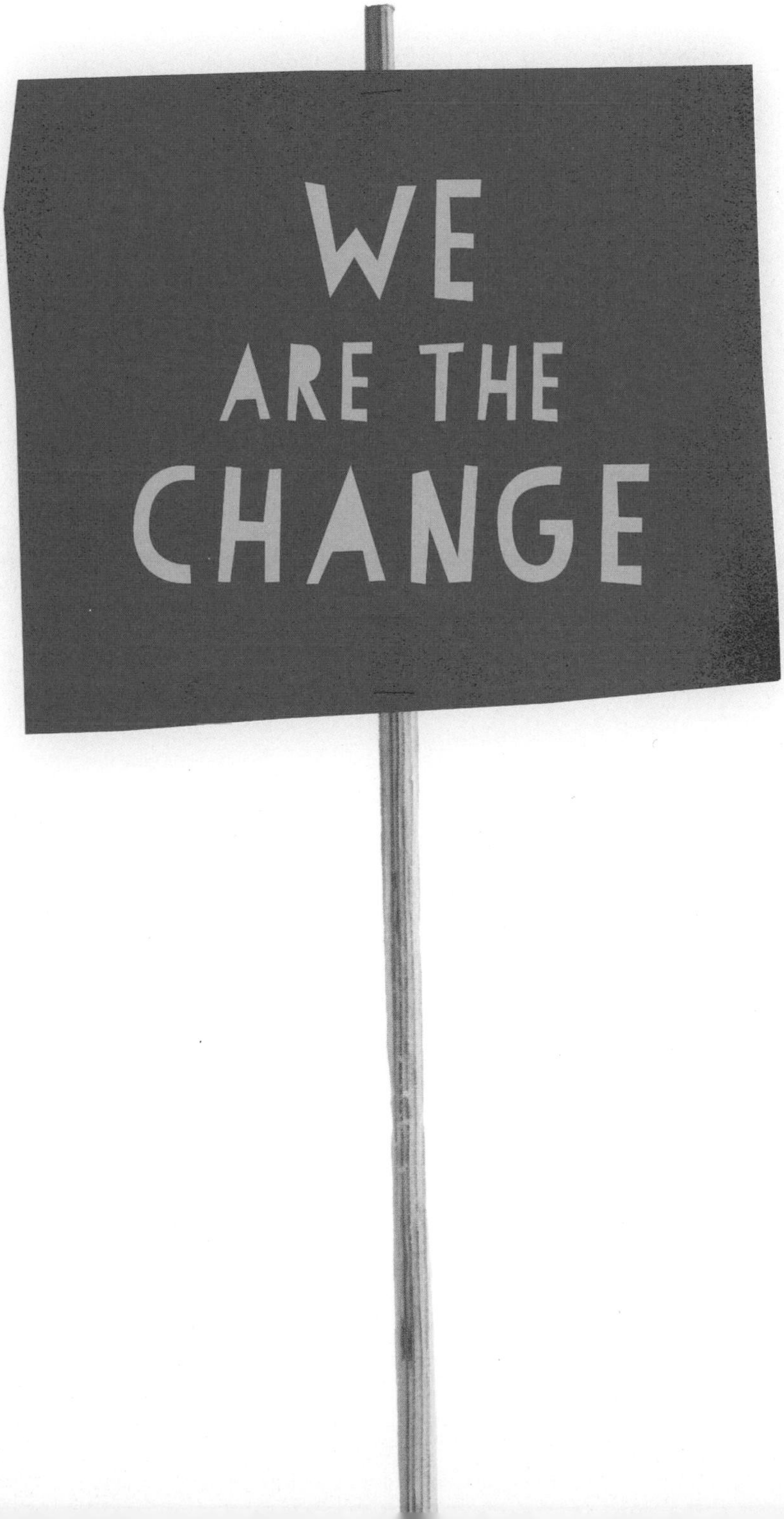
WE
ARE THE
CHANGE

**WITH ART FROM:**
Selina Alko
Alina Chau
Lisa Congdon
Emily Hughes
Molly Idle
Juana Medina
Innosanto Nagara
Christopher Silas Neal
John Parra
Brian Pinkney
Greg Pizzoli
Sean Qualls
Dan Santat
Shadra Strickland
Melissa Sweet
Raúl the Third

# WE ARE THE CHANGE

## WORDS OF INSPIRATION FROM CIVIL RIGHTS LEADERS

With an introduction by **HARRY BELAFONTE**

*chronicle books*
*san francisco*

FSC
www.fsc.org

MIX
Paper from
responsible sources
FSC™ C136333

This book was inspired by the continuing work of the
AMERICAN CIVIL LIBERTIES UNION,
which guards the rights of all Americans under law.

"So long as we have enough
people in this country willing
to fight for their rights,
we'll be called a democracy."

—AMERICAN CIVIL LIBERTIES UNION FOUNDER ROGER BALDWIN

# TABLE OF CONTENTS

# INTRODUCTION

When the founders of our country wrote the Constitution, they began with three revolutionary words: *We the People*. They began with the extraordinary idea that the future of a country is its people's future—and their fate will be its fate.

This is an idea that invests in citizenship a profound majesty, an individual dignity, and a lifelong responsibility of each man and woman to one another.

This is an idea that invests in equality the assurance that when opportunity is shared, it does not divide but rather multiplies, advancing the horizons of each individual and each industry.

This is an idea that testifies powerfully to the truth that when we turn our backs on one another, we turn the world against us, and we leave ourselves each to fight alone . . . but that when every man and woman's plight is our plight, then we find at every hand brothers and sisters to fight for us, and at our sides.

This idea—*e pluribus unum*—out of many, one—insists that through our sacred bond with one another, a people can climb to a height undreamt of by the tyrannical past, and that in that light, all rights, human rights and civil rights, rights of law and rights of conscience, are, at the beginning and the end, what makes us all one, together.

Ahead of us are you, our future leaders, who will continue to learn the historical accomplishments, along with the mistakes, of our ancestors. Take this opportunity to explore this illustrious book highlighting some of the most influential figures in the historical fight for equality and justice.

**—HARRY BELAFONTE**

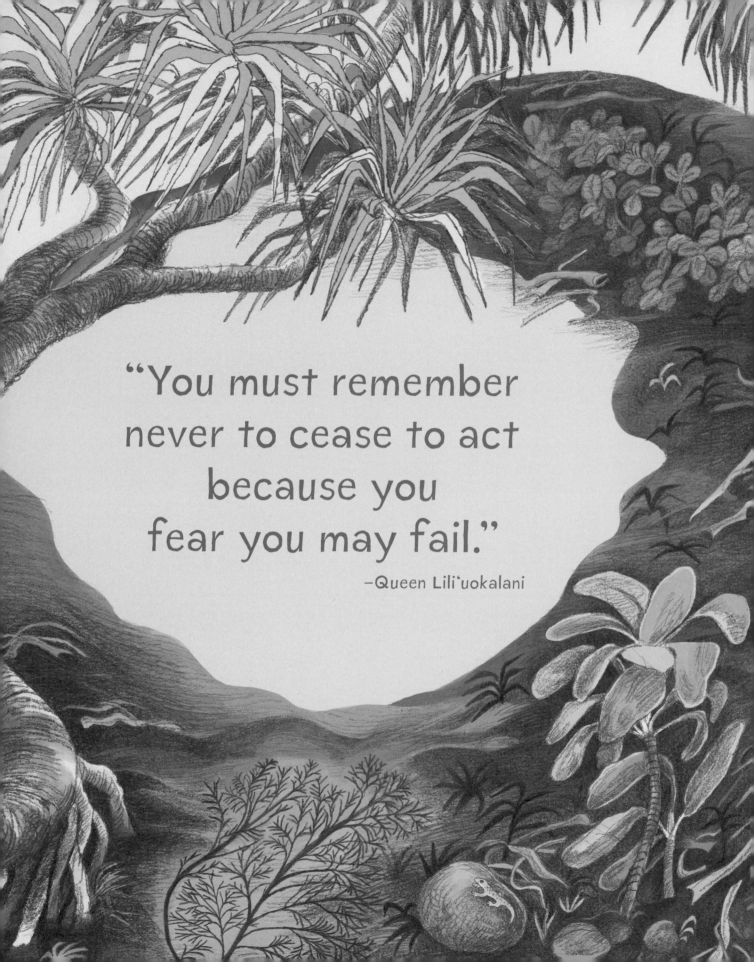

"You must remember never to cease to act because you fear you may fail."

–Queen Liliʻuokalani

**QUEEN LILI'UOKALANI DEFENDED THE RIGHTS** of her native people, her disenfranchised people, her emigrated people. Those who came to the islands were taken in as her own—received, revered, and raised as *kama'aina*, children of the land.

Lili'uokalani sacrificed her crown in order to defend what was most precious to her—respect toward life and the lives of her people. Though Hawaii's kingdom was overthrown and colonized as a part of the United States, the people she had welcomed and protected have never forgotten Lili'uokalani's strength, dignity, and encompassing love. This spirit of acceptance is not only sustained by Lili'uokalani's memory, it is a cornerstone of Hawaiian culture.

The continued custom of possessing and sharing a wide love is a fierce act of rebellion and a remembrance of the queen's deep, long-lasting wisdom.

**—EMILY HUGHES**
(on previous spread)

# PROGRESS.

**NO GREAT ADVANCE IN HUMAN RIGHTS** or social justice has ever been made without struggle. Frederick Douglass's life itself is an example of the human call to resist oppression. He endured enslavement and physical abuse and persevered to educate himself and others, fight slavery, and help lead the abolitionist movement. He is one of the most inspiring human beings of the last 200 years and is for me a shining symbol of courage and determination!

**—LISA CONGDON**
(on following spread)

IF THERE IS
NO STRUGGLE
THERE IS NO
PROGRESS.
—FREDERICK DOUGLASS

"WE MAY NOT HAVE CHOSEN THE TIME,

BUT THE TIME HAS CHOSEN US."

—JOHN LEWIS

**WHEN I WAS A KID**, it used to be considered rude to ask someone who they voted for, and I see a lot of the division in this nation stemming from the fact that this no longer applies. These days, many people wear their political views proudly, but not all of us are comfortable being outspoken in political action.

Even this very book you are holding will be assessed with a certain political view of its intentions. Some may love it, others may detest it, but no matter how you choose to exist in this nation, there is no right or wrong answer but the freedom to be vocal with your vote. John Lewis was famous for getting into "good trouble," and I have always found his actions of protest during the civil rights movement of the 1960s and up until today to be very inspirational.

I am not as brave as John Lewis is—brave enough to use my body in order to fight for a cause. I do, however, have the power to vote, which is the most powerful tool Americans have to create change in this country. Voting is a way for a quiet voice like my own to be heard no matter how outspoken others may be. We may not find ourselves in a time that is ideal for our needs and interests, but with the power to vote we can create change for our good and the greater good, and to shape this great nation to serve all its voices.

—DAN SANTAT
(on previous spread)

# "JUST LIKE MOONS AND LIKE SUNS, WITH THE CERTAINTY OF TIDES, JUST LIKE HOPES SPRINGING HIGH, STILL I'LL RISE."

—MAYA ANGELOU

**CIVIL RIGHTS ARE HUMAN RIGHTS**, to which all people are entitled, and are as natural as the sun and moon. Maya Angelou's poem, "Still I Rise," is a proclamation of every person's right to self-definition and self-determination despite what oppressive forces may suggest otherwise. I like to think of it as an anthem for every person.

**—SEAN QUALLS**
(on following spread)

"Darkness cannot drive out darkness.
Only light can do that.
Hate cannot drive out hate.
Only love can do that."

–Dr. Martin Luther King Jr.

**THIS QUOTATION APPLIES** to the importance of bringing light to nations, communities, and the lives of individuals. Illuminating disturbing situations can offer understanding, hope, awareness, and change. One of the purest forms of light is love. Applying a loving approach to difficult interactions is the answer to resolving them peacefully. This is especially true when discrimination or racism inflicts darkness and attempts to shroud love's powerful brilliance. There is even light within the human heart. That light— manifesting as love—has the capacity to heal hatred.

We need this reminder today. Especially now.

And always.

**—BRIAN PINKNEY**

"Where, after all, do universal human rights begin? In small places, close to home—so close and so small that they cannot be seen on any map of the world."

—Eleanor Roosevelt

**THE WORLD AND ALL OF ITS PROBLEMS** can seem so very big . . . and that can make each one of us feel so very small and alone. And when we feel alone, it is easy to think there is little that any one of us can do to help. But these words by Eleanor Roosevelt remind me that even the smallest acts of kindness can help make the world a better place. After all, the lines drawn on maps to divide us into nations, states, and towns are only imaginary. The little place I call home is next door to another home, which is next door to another home, and another and another, and many, many more, that lead to *your* little home. We are all connected—so we are never truly alone. And all of us, together, little by little, can make this big world a better place.

**—MOLLY IDLE**
(on previous spread)

ELEANOR ROOSEVELT ▲ illustrated by MOLLY IDLE

18

**IN TIMES OF DIVISIVENESS**, the words of Gwendolyn Brooks fill me with eagerness to find common ground with others. Yes, there will always be differences among us, but keeping present the notion of how WE are here together, all yearning for connection, makes me believe that hard conversations are worth our time and effort.

Just as harvesting takes true dedication, patience, and care, conversations won't bear fruit immediately. But little by little, if we give our best, we will be able to see our bond grow.

**—JUANA MEDINA**
(on following spread)

"We are each other's harvest;
we are each other's business;
we are each other's magnitude and bond."

—Gwendolyn Brooks

# "IF THE SYSTEM IS BROKEN, MY INCLINATION IS TO FIX IT RATHER THAN TO FIGHT IT."

—SONIA SOTOMAYOR

**THERE IS CALL TO ACTION** in Supreme Court Justice Sonia Sotomayor's words. Often, the process of solving large systematic issues is not easy. It involves planning, determination, cooperation, and hard work. Sometimes, in order to stay focused, we need to begin with small steps to address a problem. Sotomayor's words remind us that we can accomplish much by reframing our goals of working toward what we believe in, instead of what we are against.

—JOHN PARRA

"People have a right to different opinions, but those differences should not turn into hatred. We should love and care for each other because we are all one human race."

—Dolores Huerta

**AS A YOUNG BOY**, I knew that my family was different than the American families portrayed on the TV, in books, and in movies. I knew that I was made to feel less than American because my mother didn't speak English. I knew that certain people looked at me with suspicion because they had been taught to believe that I might be dangerous. And for the longest time I didn't realize that these opinions had created walls that were being used against me and others like me, and keeping us from achieving our true potential. It took a long time to overcome the obstacles and feelings of insecurity that these opinions had formed within me, and today when I look back at them as an adult I know that I was fortunate to survive and to become the artist that I am today.

So when I hear our own leaders fill the air with racist remarks, I know that a new generation of kids is going to grow up feeling unwelcome and less than human, and it breaks my heart; but I hope that these times will pass and that we can begin to heal our youth—to make them feel loved and at home.

**—RAÚL THE THIRD**

# THERE IS BUT ONE COWARD ON EARTH

AND THAT IS THE COWARD THAT
DARE NOT KNOW
- W. E. B. Du Bois
ALL ARE EQUAL
PROTECT THE SMALL
AM I NEXT?
LOVE TRUMPS HATE
UNITED WE STAND
DISSENT IS PATRIOTIC
WE SHALL OVERCOME

**I DON'T WANT TO BE A COWARD.** I want to be brave.
I don't want to look away. But at times, and nowadays
it's quite often, things seem so bad, so overwhelmingly
bad, that looking away seems the only option. It's not.
There is protest, there is charity, there is action. This
quote resonated with me for two reasons: it calls out
those in power who refuse to acknowledge the rights
and liberties of the powerless, and it also asks all of us
to recognize how we are complicit in the problems to
which we are oblivious or that we choose to overlook.
I am happy to contribute artwork for this edition and
to support the work that the ACLU does to ensure that
the voices those in power "dare not know" are known,
and heard.

**—GREG PIZZOLI**
(on previous spread)

ALL
ARE
EQUAL

**I AM A JEWISH WOMAN** from Canada, mother to two biracial children, each of them beautiful and strong. Now I live in Brooklyn, New York, and I meet people from all over the world in the schools that I visit, the libraries I go to, the subways I ride on, and the streets that I walk down. My work as an illustrator is to capture the world around me, to not only show what I see but what I feel needs to be seen. There is power in creating imagery. I have always intuitively felt beauty and strength in representing different cultures, perspectives, and points of view. Life would be really bland if we only knew and told our own stories.

—SELINA ALKO

(on following spread)

"IN DIVERSITY THERE IS BEAUTY AND THERE IS STRENGTH."

—MAYA ANGELOU

"I am a member of a party of one . . . I hold it that it would be improper for any committee or any employer to examine my conscience. . . . It is not a crime to believe anything at all in America."

—E. B. White

We the People  of the Uni

4. Proofs that the Earth is round.—I.

Four score and seven years a brought forth on this contine

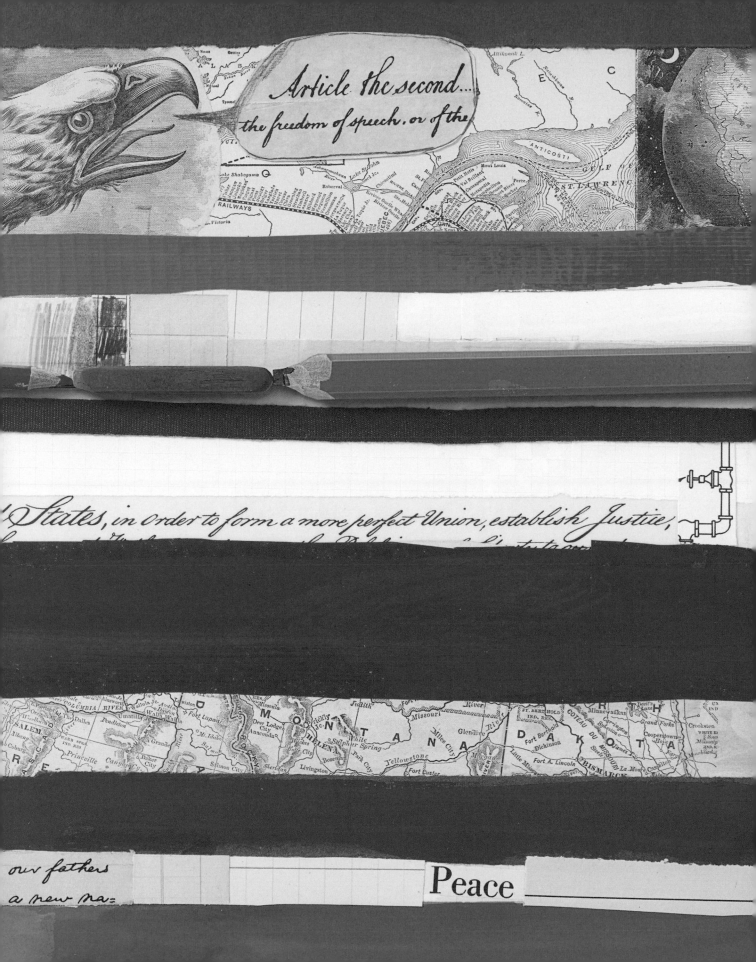

**E. B. WHITE WROTE THIS QUOTE** in 1947, in response to those who refused to answer questions before the House Un-American Activities Committee. This committee was charged with uncovering (assumed) anti-American, disloyal, pro-communist, or subversive efforts. (This practice later became known as "McCarthyism" because Senator Joseph McCarthy championed the cause.)

Many of those investigated were writers and other artists, and a number of them were "blacklisted"— their names put on a list of people to be avoided, refused employment, or fired from their jobs. Even when the blacklisting was over, some never rebuilt their careers.

Throughout E. B. White's life he stood for democracy and, as a writer, believed profoundly in the freedom of speech. His quote reminds me that the power of being an artist lies in freedom of expression. White's conviction inspires me to ensure my work expresses any idea I believe in, subversive or otherwise.

—MELISSA SWEET
(on previous spread)

**I CHOSE THIS EXCERPT** from Khalil Gibran's poem "On Children" because I feel it is a beautiful articulation of an idea that is at the foundation of all civil rights: that no person belongs to you, body or mind, including your children. Especially our children—as they are the most powerless in their relationship to both us and the state. Yet "their souls dwell in the house of tomorrow, which you cannot visit, not even in your dreams." The choices we make today must protect our children's right to determine their own path into that future that they will be living (we hope) long beyond our own time. I write children's books that aim in some small way to give children and their families a forum to explore social justice issues, and to understand the agency they have to participate in the shaping of their world. Indeed, we are responsible for making many choices on our children's behalf until they are able to themselves. Thus it is all the more important that we adults also fiercely defend their right to their own dreams and that we protect the possibility that they make those dreams a reality.

—INNOSANTO NAGARA
(on following spread)

"Your children are not your children.
They are the sons and daughters of Life's longing for itself.
They come through you but not from you,
And though they are with you yet they belong not to you.

You may give them your love but not your thoughts,
For they have their own thoughts.
You may house their bodies but not their souls,
For their souls dwell in the house of tomorrow,
which you cannot visit, not even in your dreams."

—Khalil Gibran

"I'll tell you what freedom is to me: no fear."

—Nina Simone

NINA SIMONE IS KNOWN for her incredible talent as a pianist and singer, but rarely is she showcased as a civil rights activist. I have always admired her unforgettable protest music, and now, with digital access to many of her interviews via the internet, it is apparent just how much she sacrificed for the civil rights movement. I was introduced to her music as a teenager and have been obsessed with her ever since. She was a champion for young black people especially—wanting us to know the beauty and power that we all hold in spite of what the world shouts back at us. One of her most popular songs, "To Be Young, Gifted and Black" (1970), is an unapologetic anthem for young black people across the world. It is a great honor contributing this work in her memory.

—SHADRA STRICKLAND

(on previous spread)

NINA SIMONE ▲ illustrated by SHADRA STRICKLAND

**MY MOM GAVE ME A BOOK**—a biography—about Helen Keller when I was six years old. In it I read about how, suffering from a mysterious illness, Helen Keller lost her sight and hearing at a young age. Yet her perseverance triumphed over these disadvantages—she achieved academic success, and she became an advocate for people with disabilities, for women's rights, for social equality, and for pacifism. Her courage and optimism have been an inspiration to me since I was a child.

I wanted to capture Helen Keller's joyful spirit toward life. The dove and olive branch symbolize peace; the characters represent the togetherness she believed in—a beautiful, diverse group of citizens and custodians of our planet, who as individuals contribute each in a small way, yet as a group are making the world a happier place for future generations.

**—ALINA CHAU**
(on following spread)

HELEN KELLER ▶ illustrated by **ALINA CHAU**

"Alone we can do so little;
together we can do so much."

—Helen Keller

"Change will not come
if we wait for some other
person or some other time.

We are the ones
we've been waiting for.

# WE ARE THE CHANGE
# THAT WE SEEK."

—Barack Obama

**I FEEL EMPOWERED** hearing Barack Obama's words. If there's something we want, whether it's changing something about our own life or creating world peace, Obama reminds us that within each of us lie the strength and tools to make it happen. We can build our own wings.

**—CHRISTOPHER SILAS NEAL**

# ILLUSTRATOR BIOGRAPHIES

**SELINA ALKO** has always been curious about different people and cultures, which stems, in part, from growing up with a Canadian mother and with a Turkish father who spoke seven languages and taught her to paint. Her art brims with optimism, experimentation, and a deep commitment to multiculturalism and human rights. She is the author of *The Case for Loving*, which she illustrated with her husband, Sean Qualls; and the co-illustrator, also with Sean, of *Why Am I Me?* by Paige Britt and *Two Friends* by Dean Robbins. She has written and illustrated several other acclaimed picture books, including *Daddy Christmas & Hanukkah Mama* and *B Is for Brooklyn*. She lives in Brooklyn, New York, with her family. Learn more at www.selinaalko.com.

**ALINA CHAU** grew up in Hong Kong, where she discovered that drawing and painting were the best way to keep herself out of mischief, which eventually led her to the United States and to an MFA from University of California, Los Angeles, School of Theater, Film and Television. After over a decade working in the animation industry, she focused on illustration and writing stories full time. Her whimsical art style is highly sought after for art exhibits worldwide. Alina Chau currently resides in Los Angeles with her mischievous puppy, Piglet.

**LISA CONGDON** is an author, illustrator, and fine artist, best known for her colorful paintings and drawings and her quirky hand lettering. Her books include *A Glorious Freedom: Older Women Leading Extraordinary Lives*; *Whatever You Are, Be a Good One*; *Art, Inc.: The Essential Guide to Building Your Career as an Artist*; *Fortune Favors the Brave*; and *The Joy of Swimming*. She was named one of *Forty Women to Watch Over 40* in 2015 and she is featured in the 2017 book *200 Women Who Will Change the Way You See the World*. She lives in Portland, Oregon. You can see more of her work at www.lisacongdon.com.

**EMILY HUGHES** is an Asian American illustrator currently living and drawing in London, England. She is the recipient of the 2018 Geisel Medal with Laurel Snyder for *Charlie & Mouse*. Her books include *Wild* and *The Little Gardener*, and illustrations done for Sean Taylor's *A Brave Bear* and Carter Higgins's *Everything You Need for a Treehouse*. Much of her work is influenced by the natural world, stemming from memories of her family and childhood in Hilo, Hawaii.

**MOLLY IDLE** is the Caldecott Honor–winning illustrator of *Flora and the Flamingo*. She is also the creator of *Flora and the Penguin*, *Flora and the Peacocks*, and the Rex series—which includes *Tea Rex*, *Camp Rex*, and *Sea Rex*. Molly lives and works with her fabulous family in Tempe, Arizona, where she can be found with a cup of espresso in one hand and a pencil in the other, scribbling away on her next book. To learn more about Molly and her work visit www.idleillustration.com.

**JUANA MEDINA** is the author and illustrator of *1 Big Salad*, *ABC Pasta*, *Sweet Shapes*, and the 2017 Pura Belpré Award winner, *Juana & Lucas*. She also illustrated *Smick!* written by Doreen Cronin. Juana has studied and taught at the Rhode Island School of Design and the Corcoran School of the Arts & Design. She lives in Washington, D.C., with her wife, twin sons, and their dear dog, Rosita. Visit her at www.juanamedina.com.

**INNOSANTO NAGARA** was born and raised in Jakarta, Indonesia, and came to the United States to study zoology and philosophy at UC Davis. He then moved to the San Francisco Bay Area, where he worked as a graphic designer for a range of activist projects before founding Design Action Collective, a worker-owned design studio serving the movement for social justice. His journey as a children's book author and illustrator began with the surprise bestseller *A Is for Activist*. He has since written and illustrated a number of other "new wave" children's books with social justice and activist themes: *Counting on Community*, *My Night in the Planetarium*, and *The Wedding Portrait*. His fifth book, an illustrated chapter book about what makes a movement, will be coming out in the Fall of 2019.

**CHRISTOPHER SILAS NEAL** is an award-winning illustrator and author who regularly contributes to the *New York Times* and *The New Yorker*, and creates book covers for various publishers. He has directed short animated videos for Kate Spade and Anthropologie, and was awarded a medal from the Society of Illustrators for his work in motion graphics.

He illustrated the acclaimed picture books *Over and Under the Snow* and *Lifetime*, both of which explore the natural world. *Over and Under the Snow*, with author Kate Messner, was praised for its "stunning retro-style illustrations" (*New York Times*); it was a 2011 *New York Times* Editor's Choice and won an E. B. White Honor Award in 2012. He recently contributed art to *New York Times* bestseller *Goodnight Songs*, a collection of poems by the author of *Goodnight Moon*, Margaret Wise Brown. Christopher's authorial debut, *Everyone*, is available now.

JOHN PARRA is an award-winning illustrator, designer, and educator, best known for his illustrated Latino-themed children's books such as *Waiting for the Biblioburro*, *Green Is a Chile Pepper*, and *Gracias/Thanks*. His recognitions include the SCBWI Golden Kite Award, ALA's Pura Belpré Honors, the Christopher Award, and the International Latino Book Award. His illustration clients have included United Airlines, Hitachi Data, Jeep/Chrysler Motors, National Geographic, PBS, Boston's

Children's Hospital, Chronicle Books, Penguin Random House, Simon and Schuster, and Virgin Records. Parra's original artwork has also been showcased and displayed in numerous gallery shows and museum exhibitions in New York, California, and throughout the United States and abroad. Many of his fine art paintings now reside with private collectors. In 2015 John was invited by the Metropolitan Museum of Art in New York to present a special event about his work and career in art and illustration; and in 2017 his work was seen at the U.S. Post Office on six new Forever Stamps titled *Delicioso*, with art celebrating Latino cuisine. John's recent children's book, *Frida Kahlo and Her Animalitos*, was selected as one of the winners of the *New York Times*/New York Public Library Best Illustrated Children's Books of 2017 and received an ALA Pura Belpré Honor as well. Today, John lives with his wife, Maria, in Queens, New York. To learn more visit www.johnparraart.com.

In addition to two Caldecott Honors, BRIAN PINKNEY has also been awarded the Boston Globe–Horn Book Award, a Coretta Scott King Award, and four Coretta Scott King Honors. Whenever he sets a goal he taps into his inner animal, and he credits an active and playful imagination as a key to his success in sports, art, and life. Brian lives in Brooklyn, New York, with his wife and frequent collaborator, Andrea Davis Pinkney, and their two children. www.brianpinkney.net.

**GREG PIZZOLI** is the author and illustrator of several picture books including *The Watermelon Seed*, *Good Night Owl*, and *This Story Is for You*. His artwork is featured in many other books, including the Jack series by Mac Barnett, the My Little Cities series by Jennifer Adams, and *North, South, East, West* by Margaret Wise Brown. He lives in Philadelphia.

**SEAN QUALLS** finds inspiration everywhere, from old buildings, nature, fairy tales, black memorabilia, and outsider art to cave paintings, African imagery, mythology, music, and his native Brooklyn. He is the co-illustrator, with his wife, Selina Alko, of the celebrated picture books *Two Friends* by Dean Robbins and *The Case for Loving*, also written by Selina Alko. Other acclaimed picture books he has illustrated include *Giant Steps to Change the World* by Spike Lee and Tonya Lewis Lee; *Little Cloud and Lady Wind* by Toni Morrison and her son Slade; *Dizzy* by Jonah Winter; and *Before John Was a Jazz Giant* by Car-

ole Boston Weatherford, for which he received a Coretta Scott King Illustrator Honor. He lives in Brooklyn, New York, with his family. Visit him online at www.seanqualls.com.

**DAN SANTAT** is the Caldecott Medal-winning and *New York Times*-bestselling author and illustrator of *The Adventures of Beekle: The Unimaginary Friend* and the road trip/time travel adventure *Are We There Yet?* His artwork is also featured in numerous picture books, chapter books, and middle-grade novels, including Dav Pilkey's Ricky Ricotta series. Dan lives in Southern California with his wife, two kids, and many, many pets.

**SHADRA STRICKLAND** is an illustrator whose work includes *Loving vs. Virginia*, *Bird*, and *A Child's Book of Prayers and Blessings*. She has won an Ezra Jack Keats Award, a Coretta Scott King/ John Steptoe Award for New Talent, and an NAACP Image Award. She is also a professor of illustration at the Maryland Institute College of Art.

**MELISSA SWEET** is a collage artist obsessed with the alphabet in any form. She has written and illustrated many award-winning books including

*Balloons Over Broadway: The True Story of the Puppeteer of Macy's Parade*, a Sibert Medal winner; two Caldecott Honor–winning books, *The Right Word* and *A River of Words*, both by Jen Bryant; and *Little Red Writing* by Joan Holub.

Melissa wrote and illustrated *Some Writer! The Story of E. B. White*, a *New York Times* bestseller, which garnered the National Council of Teachers of English Orbis Pictus Award for nonfiction and a Boston Globe–Horn Book Honor. She brings her favorite quote by E. B. White to the studio each day: "Be tidy. Be brave."

Reviewers have described Melissa's unique mixed-media illustrations as "exuberant," "outstanding," and "a creative delight." When she's not in her studio she can be found riding her red Schwinn bicycle around Portland, Maine, with her dog, Ruby.

RAÚL THE THIRD teaches classes on drawing and comics for kids at the Museum of Fine Arts and the Institute of Contemporary Art in Boston, Massachusetts, where he lives. He is the illustrator of the graphic novel Lowriders series, written by Cathy Camper.

"You must remember never to cease to act because you fear you may fail."

—Queen Lili'uokalani